EULOGY FOR AN IMPERFECT MAN

2-16-13

Judy,

Eulogy for an Imperfect Man

Poems by Maureen A. Sherbondy

Best wishes.

Maureen Sh

BRICK ROAD

POETRY PRESS

Cover photo: "Father and Daughter" ©iStockphoto.com/Claudiad

Author photo: Tom Edwards, New Image Studio, Raleigh

Library of Congress Control Number: 2012938670
ISBN-13: 978-0-9835304-3-5

Published by Brick Road Poetry Press
P. O. Box 751
Columbus, GA 31902-0751
www.brickroadpoetrypress.com

Brick Road logo by Dwight New

For my brothers
David, Jonathan, and Bruce

The author wishes to thank the editors of Brick Road Poetry Press,
her wonderful poetry group, the students and faculty
of Queens University of Charlotte, the NCPS, the NCWN,
her "open mic" pals, Sharon Kurtzman, Therese Fowler,
Janet Silber, Susan Dreyfus, Johnnye Locke, Jane Elkins,
Diane Chamberlain, Jodi Barnes, Robin Miura, Jan Parker,
Malaika King Albrecht, Anne Barnhill, the Kadish and Buxbaum
families, and, most of all, Jacob, Ethan, and Zachary.

CONTENTS

The Gods of Grief

Eulogy for an Imperfect Man

Grief Collage

Death ends a life, not a relationship.

—Robert Benchley

The Gods of Grief

Dust

Those who sleep in the dust
have seen better days.
Gray specks veil sealed
eyes, mouths, and legs.

Once they could feel the palm
of a child's hand curled inside
their own live hand.

Decades they glided
or shuddered through
life's wild trials. Once they could rise
from this state and spit out
the seeded dust of sleep and memory
and walk above the grass and dirt.

Once they could bleed.

Those who sleep in the dust
have seen better days. They only wake
when the letters of their names are caressed
against the lips of the living.
They shake off the suit of ash,
and rise up again.

Calling the Dead

My friend dials her mother's number
out of habit, then remembers,
My mother is dead!
Again. The shock of it.

Maybe we should call the departed,
a lost mother number assigned
to the grieving. The phone rings;
someone answers and just listens.

So we can say all those things we meant
to say but could not,
tell the listener how our lives are
while we adjust to absence

slowly, until we learn to wean ourselves
from our mothers, when we can
dip our toes inside
this cold ocean of loss.

Father-Daughter Dance

It's her wedding day,
he leads, she follows, they laugh
and sail across the marble floor.

She is waltzing with her father,
not the wicked, rejecting one,
but the father she always imagined,

Until the stars appear
here, where marriage lasts forever
and fathers never die.

The Gods of Grief

The gods have gone deaf
in their old age and lost
their memory too.

They do not hear my voice
or recall their old promises
inscribed in stone.

Are they blind too—
unable to see what
has transpired beneath

the moon and stars?
Perhaps they are so uninspired
in their high towers

and merely playing
out the drama with survivors,
seeking to understand

through remote witness
the very meaning
of grief.

What We Bury

What did you bury
behind the willow tree,
beyond the rusted swing set?

Remember the thin baby bird
fallen from its nest? You brought it worms,
trickled water from a dropper.
It didn't seem such a long topple down
to cause that twisted neck.

You didn't understand
why it closed its dark eyes
like rain-glazed stones buried in sand.
Dad dug a hand-deep hole,
covered the feathers with dirt.

What did you bury in your yard?
Hard seeds smaller than your
dirt-edged finger nails.
Dad sprinkled dirt again.
Set it down, he whispered softly
and you did.

Elm trees grew inside the yard

after spring's sudden splatter of rain,

and you waited for that bird

to sprout back up,

to lift and fly from the soil,

but it never did.

Harvest

When the living die
in Minnesota during winter,
what becomes of them?

Do gravediggers warm the earth
with breath or flame, weld
open a resting place?

Or, perhaps grave planners
estimate the holes,
study last year's obituary
section and take a census,
then pre-dig enough
openings in spring when the thaw
of earth allows for dirt removal.

I picture rows and rows of neat rectangles,
a farmer preparing his field, setting
a place to bury the seeds
so the living can rise from this same
earth come harvest time.

When the corpses of the deceased
are buried finally, covered with

frozen dirt, I wonder what crop

we will reap from this last planting.

Merchant Afterlife

On price stickers for the dead
to view, dollars have been crossed out,
everything is free here, bins
filled with merchandise, loss, despair.
The dead walk bare,
their flesh left behind
in boxes in the ground.

Still,
the merchant cannot abandon his desire
to sell. Memory and routine cling
and chafe even after life. T-shirts for a smile,
socks for a nod, Timex watches with stopped hands
given out anyway while spiel slips
from ghostly sales lips. He invents new uses for
the useless. Twenty-four-hour shopping network
host for heaven, hell, and limbo too.

Words coat his slick tongue, an old song
comforting him in his loss; he says nay to the spiritual,
his trinity is hook, pitch, then close the deal,
the familiar art of persuasion—an old friend,
his escort through eternity.

Loose Coffins in Carolina

Flood waters rise, dams leak
cemeteries give up their dead.
Do you see the long-buried coffins
floating down Main Street?
Even time cannot hold the departed.

Bones of Smith and Jones drift boxed,
pass the (flooded) coffee shop.
Maybe they want to return
to this place again,
where misery increases
as the Tar River abandons its erased edges.

Work crews torch piles of pigs,
sending plumes of wood-hog smoke·up
in clouds, to pose the question:
who will come to this
southern pig pickin', while
the natives all stand stranded on roofs?

How do you bury the dead
when the ground won't allow it,
when it won't even show itself,

when the once hard surface

is drowning in water

and will hold nothing down?

See the pigs floating, the chickens too;

see the bodies. Now where is that ark?

Accidentally Caught
in a Funeral Procession

Caught accidentally in this final line—
funeral procession of cars,
red flashers on, trooper lights
leading the flock of metal-shelled
mourners, passengers clutching tissues
soaked with tears.

I pass through the red lights too,
wonder would it be rude
to change lanes now, depart from pain.
Would this be a traffic violation
of the dead? What is the proper
etiquette in a situation such as this?

I follow loss to road's end.
It travels forward, bumper to bumper,
plateaus at the cemetery, as the coffin lowers.
No one asks why I am there.
We cry, share, and breathe in
the same outdoor sorrowful air.

December Shiva

The house is thick with grief,
thirty mourners and
no one will say how
the younger brother died.

I want to know
in this house thick with grief,
but the question whispered
in the kitchen feels like gossip,

dangles unanswered,
creeps into the life equation.
In this house thick with grief,
no mention of heart attack, embolism,

accident. I picture hanging,
self-inflicted gunshot wound
in this house thick with grief.
The woman I ask shakes her head,

turns away. The Mourner's Kaddish
minyan of chanters cry

in this house thick with grief

when the sister reminisces

aloud about the dead man, his grieving children,

three of them, ten years old and younger.

Sobs rise up, can't find solace

in this house so thick with grief.

I skip coffee cake and baklava,

exit the front door, shoulders weighed

down with grief—those fatherless children,

the widow's empty bed.

Independent Living

Twenty years later
she's suddenly aware
all seventy-four residents
have passed on
from that retirement home
where she once worked,

filling out papers,
accounting for each life,
leading craft activities,
transporting them
from Royal Vista Terrace
to the store and back again.

She sees seventy-four empty beds.
No more sweet Katherine, or spunky Beverly,
or sad Ruth. Not even that stubborn Edith,
the annoying one who made
a sport out of argument. Did she
fight death until the end?

Their wrinkled faces drift by
at night, float through her dreams,

and a spoken line lingers even now
in the warm North Carolina summer air.

Mostly, she recalls them gathering
in the main lobby, sitting
in those high-backed chairs waiting
for the mailman, for letters
and junk mail, this final delivery.

One Year after Your Death

When I find out you have died
I die a little, too,
a gasp escapes, a squall of grief.
For weeks

I contemplate June
one year before.
How could I not have sensed
your departure?

That was the day I arrived
at my island sanctuary
of sand and oat grass,
maritime forest and ocean.

Was there a moment, a notion
as I rocked back and forth
upon the front porch that evening,
reading, pondering, or humming

when a yellow bird perched
itself upon a twisted oak tree's branch?
It stared at me, whistled
its dirge into the ocean breeze.

Or, perhaps an anole
quietly darted
across the deck, taking with him
his subtle motion-coded message.

Where were my muses then?

There was just this—
the splash
of one more wave crashing
and foaming upon the sand.

The high-pitched call from
a sea bird's mouth,
saltwater pulling a handful
of sandy grains back

into the ocean. That lost wave
ever so slightly changing the shape
of the sandy beach, so subtle a shift
no one noticed it, not even me.

No News

I thought someone would tell me,
deliver news of your death,
notify me across state lines
in a neat, white-sealed envelope,
tap out a code from there to here.

Not a single clue.
No black cat strutted back and forth
across my lawn, just this
cursor blinking your name
beside a pregnant 'D'
for deceased.

It's my fault, losing touch,
can't remember why—
marriage, babies, jobs.
All these excuses now buried
with you. Wish I could say
good-bye. This word
I took for granted locked
now inside my throat.

Eulogy for an Imperfect Man

Rehash

Brother, when we speak
of our shared childhood,
the bright room grows dim.

There in the corner is
our drunken father, blacked out
on the couch in that basement
apartment off Route One.

How is it that we are nearing
the age he was then?
When memory leaves
our adult tongues,
we become those same
neglected children again.

Box Salesman

He didn't even make the boxes;
he sold them
in reds and greens, blues and whites.
He didn't design them
or even fold them.
He told suited men
in charge of purchasing
he could box the clouds
if need be.

He sold exteriors, perimeters
like how he always paced the periphery,
making rectangular patterns around the yard,
inspecting grass and house
from remote, outside edges.
Sometimes he stepped onto the lawn
to take away branch from tree,
to plant seeds, to plant four children.

But mostly, he was pacing the outside
until he got so far away
Mom pushed him out for good.
All that remained

were those cases of boxes,

boxes holding

nothing.

After a Visit

Father, I see him—
Death hovering
above your shoulders,
behind your pale skin,
your gray eyes,
light already fading.

Clouds announce the end
of you and me
and this swatch of place
we have made.

And I want to tell you
so many things,
but words stall
and die flat on my tongue—
words I've never been able
to birth and release.

Not this day,
but soon, when another moon
slips away, there will be
a universe of space

between us. Maybe then

these words will spill

out and rise up

toward your shadow.

Only Daughter

I confess, I was never daddy's little princess
never had him
wrapped around
my girly fingertips.

I was off running with the boys of summer
playing with Tonka trucks, soccer balls,
not playing jacks, house, or *The Dating Game.*

Tried to be what he admired.
Girls were just a mystery,
like a foreign plant he did not know
when to shade or water.
I was the only daughter.

And when I grew into a satin, sequined
bride, it was the same, he hid.
Did not know how to give
me away, had no gems of advice
to say. When he lifted my veil,
sheer cover of a stranger,
the unknown revealed,
he gave me away—relief
in his eyes, not elation or adoration.

He didn't choose to twirl me around

in that father-daughter wedding dance,

so, with my groom, I swirled out of the room.

How could I ask for more than he could give?

I was never daddy's little princess.

What They Will Find after He's Gone

Chilled vodka bottles
stored in the freezer,
his son's paintings hung
on dusty townhouse walls,
that one gold wedding band
not worn in thirty-five years
hiding in the sock drawer,
creased letters from an old girlfriend,
photos of long-dead relatives,
and that deep indentation
in the couch where he sat
for decades entertained by sports,
watching other people play and live,
as his own life limped by,
his body anchored to that one spot
on the worn seat cushion.

Sorry

After my brother called
from miles away to relay
the end of our father's life,
over and over I simply said,

Sorry

To the bedroom air, the walls
of my house, to the longleaf pines
outside and the thin layer
of snow coating the yard and deck.

This Day

The morning my father passes
I stumble outside,
step wobbly through the shock
of February's last winter spell,

lift up the newspaper
as I do every day
even this one, attempting to
insulate my grief with routine.

Then, walking back to the house
green—
four stalks, like four siblings
side by side by side by side
rising through this
unforgiving ground.

The Dead, Phone

Of course the phones
in Queens went dead
the day my dad stopped
breathing.

His only sister sat
in her apartment
oblivious
to the shift in her universe.

For six hours my brother tried
to call, then he sent police
to tell her,
family emergency.

Two cops showed up,
and of course she knew,
police come to your door—
the news is never good.

Viewing

We, who cannot
get to the living
in time to say
farewell,

Lift up the wooden
lid to see that closed-eyed
face, to bid
that final good-bye.

Lids

I wanted to push back
the shade gently of his closed lids,
to see those eyes, paint
color and shape into memory.

Were they brown, or green, hazel?
In this stunned state
I could not recall the exact hue.

Most of all, I needed to know
when someone dies, does peace
or pain reflect inside those shut windows?

Meeting with the Rabbi
before the Service

My brothers' black shoes
draw a half circle.

We pin black ribbons
near our hearts and hear

the subtle sound of satin ripping,
and my father's body waits

silent in the coffin
in the other room.

Siblings

Side by side
we sit

not crying,
the shock

of sudden death
halting our tears.

Eulogy for an Imperfect Man

My brother stands up,
reads from the carefully worded speech,
struggle visible on his face.
He sticks to the facts like dots
on a map. We travel with him.

Date of birth, place of origin,
college degree, and job,
names of children,
military history,
his love of sports,
as if reciting a resumé.

We adult children in the front row
listen, nod, do not cry.
I conjure up incidents and arguments
between the lines
and the fissures on the map
not visited today.

Black-cloaked little men haunt me
in the funeral home.

These beady-eyed dark figures
peek out at me
from the margins of the eulogy.
For now I ignore them.

I am so tired.

Pallbearer

Alongside my brothers,
my teenage son holds up

my father's coffin;
he slowly slides

the simple pine box
into the long black hearse,

the future generation
pushing away the past.

Mud

The heavy mud I shoveled
into the open grave

follows me home,

weighs down the bottom
hem of my black pants.

Present Tense

I keep slipping,
using the present tense
reserved for the living

He lives in New Jersey.
He is an alcoholic.
He has four children.

My heart believes
he is still alive; my mind
tries to catch up
with this shift, one verb

Died

that has changed
every single thing.

Mirrors

Though the mirrors
were not covered
in this Reform house,

for weeks I did not look
at my image,
fearful of seeing

my own
dead father's eyes
staring back at me.

Sitting Shiva at Coffee Shops

Of course I choose this place

to sit shiva—

my usual coffee shop

with warm fireplace

and ceramic mugs.

I sink

into my customary

leather cushion

that holds years

of found words and ponderings.

Between sips of dark roast,

I spill grief upon the page

and wait for time

to lift this heavy weight.

After the Shiva

After the minyan,
when the living
room air is still
and silent, absent
of Psalm 23 and
the Mourner's Kaddish,
the grieving woman
leaves out ten chairs
gathered in a circle,
recalls her friends' faces,
their empathetic eyes,
their reaching arms
and words remaining
in the house
long after they are gone.

Trying to Have a Normal Day

This daily lashing returns
to greet me upon waking,
shakes me into remembering
he is dead.

Then fog descends, encases
my body and mind. All day
I walk into walls and forget
who I am and what I should be
doing. The umbilical threads
that once stretched out,
one to my father, one
to my mother, were cut

in the night by that large
black hand. Now I dangle
untethered from yesterday's
version of myself.

Slowly,   I   force
this body forward,
and I stumble,
and try to recall
what normal even means.

Grief Poem

Gray clouds
invade her house.

Storms begin every day;
salty rain floods each room,

climbs the walls,
the wainscoting,

and she has forgotten
how to swim.

It Will Hit You

Months later, when you are
pumping gas, or standing
in the grocery aisle,
staring at cans of peas
and beans, or in the store
sifting through
birthday cards in October,
you'll recall that he
taught you how to pump gas,
and when to change the oil,
that he, not your nervous mother,
showed you how to make stew
with beans, and while you're
buying a card for your brother,
you will feel like you forgot something,
then suddenly recall that your father's
birthday was one day after your
brother's, and this is the first
year that you won't be sending
your dad a birthday card.
And there, in the most common
everyday shop, while performing
mundane tasks, the tears

will begin, your body will shake

from shoulders to toes

and you will not be able to stop.

After Death

The weight

of each step

grows heavier, as if

while I slept

some giant hand

descended

from the clouds

and filled

my legs

with old stones

and sand.

It is easier to recline

on the couch

than to stand,

or leave this house

and lift these

grief-laden legs.

What This Grief Is Like

I want to leave
this toxic island,
but my father's voice
keeps jerking me back.

Paternal noose wrapped
around my ankles and wrists,
I am waiting
for the Phoenix to land,

lift me up and away,
but he can only locate
this place if I cry.

The tears fail to arrive,
and my dead father's palms
are still covering my lips,
silencing my voice,
and no one can hear

my muffled mutterings.

Small Birds at Night

Even though they buried him,

shoveled dirt and good-byes

upon his pine coffin, watched

the rectangular aperture

fill up with finality,

dusty remnants rose each night

from the earth. Small birds

landed on the windowsills

of his sons' and daughters' homes,

whispering

his unfinished arguments,

those lingering questions.

Each night he flew, waited

for answers, but the children

had learned years ago to sleep

with their doors and windows shut.

Bats

Death, I am so tired
of you hovering
over my house.

Like the colony of bats
in the attic
                    flitting
above our heads

at night while we try to dream,
guano lining walls and floors,
spreading disease.

Take your dark wings already,

                    leave.

Redirect

The black birds surround my car,
redirect my journey, blanket

of wings and feathers
guiding me to a place

I never intended to visit,
this dark village at the bottom

of every road, no warning sign
posted, just one exit labeled Death.

Red

Whenever I see a flaming Camaro
on the road, Exit or Stop sign,
police siren or fire truck

I think of him, hear
my mother calling *Red, Red*
through the halls of my childhood.

Fireworks bursting across July's sky,
every single Valentine's card
before my eyes. Red becomes
Red; then color is replaced by

dead.

White

I never saw my father
wearing white before,
he preferred dark clothes—
black Polo shirts, navy
pants, dark shoes.

When I view him in white
I recall my own wedding dress,
and the white-laced veil
my father lifted off my face.

The lid lifts up to reveal
his body shrouded in white
upon white, I am blinded
by the shock of it—
white clouds, white heaven,
white death.

Spring Arrives

Because you didn't believe
spring would come this year,
when daffodils open
and pollen dusts the deck yellow,
you stare and breathe in
the sweet scent drifting through
the screen door but stay inside
on this day anyway
because not long ago
someone's heart stopped,
and all you see now when you look
out your window is that coffin
lowering beneath the cold
winter ground, not yellow
flowers reaching toward the sky.

Grief Collage

Grief Collage

Grandfather, the night
before your funeral,
I slept in my mother's childhood
bed. Collages hung on the wall
all jazz and foreign faces,
city scenes patched together
and framed. Loss and grief
swirled in pieces in the darkness.

I wept, searching for answers
in the puzzle pieces of art. Fifteen.
Absence and sorrow circled
the night. Death seated
beside my slumber,
your familiar warm hand
clutching mine. A shadow
beside the sadness revealed
Here I am, I am here.

Later, I placed a stone
on your grave. Sometimes
at night I hold out my fist
and discover the edges

of stone inside.
When I open
my hand someone
squeezes back.

Potato Peel Soup

When I buy a sack of potatoes
I think of Cousin Marianna
who worked in the devil's kitchen—
in a concentration camp in Germany.

There were ten or more
to a room, she says
seeing the dirty place
in the air of present day,
the past
unable to decay and decompose.
She is peeling air away,
boiling images in her mind.

They ate potato peel soup, day after day;
once in a while she dropped a small potato
in her pocket, kept it like a memento.
She had never stolen a thing before.
Later, when her shrunken stomach hurt,
she pulled that waiting potato out,
took a bite—
hope sustained by that weight in her pocket.

She shows me her number that won't disappear.
I think about cattle branding,
about all the food even animals get,
how little she ever got.

Her dreams are filled
with nightmares.
She sees sacks and sacks of potatoes,
peels floating on top of red water,
and all those dead eyes.

Stairs at Weymouth

In that haunted writer's retreat
in Southern Pines,
a spiral staircase descended
from the ceiling.

No, it wasn't a dream.

I opened my eyes
and the corded spiral
appeared. I waited
for a ghost to show,
or a voice to whisper.

Dark hours I stared,
until early light spilled
into the room, erased
the vision.

Today I wonder
if I had it all wrong;
maybe those stairs
were waiting for me
to climb up.

Loss

During the night
autumn kitsch fell from the sky—
stiff branches, a dead tree,
acorns, and leaves.

A star, an eyelash,
a last wish.

Last night you dropped
out of my dreams—
heartbeat ceasing,
your arms reaching
to grasp the living.

Fissures invaded my universe—
when I rose, I saw holes
forming inside my yard.
No matter
where I walk
I fall in.

Mining the Obituaries

I mine the obituaries
for names,
my own sort of verbal recycling.

Life will go on for Matilda, Eugenia, Hugh,
and Felix too; only their last names change.
I'll add a fedora, or church hat, switch

their race, occupation, darken their hair,
erase some lines on their faces,
find them new lovers.

They'll visit fun places—Paris, Brussels, Rome.
I'll encourage happiness, throw
drama in, whip up some sin.

While they rest in their
new-found-beneath-the-ground addresses,
I'll make them rise up from the grave and sing.

After Running to Catch the School Bus

Tomorrow, when twelve-year-old boys and girls return to class,

students attempting to revisit the task of math,

that one empty chair hovering before them,

will they stare at emptiness, see zero?

Her name, Anusha, scrawled in permanent ink on the desk, a wad

of gum beneath the seat, a scuff on the floor where her shoe

moved back and forth between questions.

Will they miss her steady voice,

or her hand raised ready to solve an equation?

Will the teacher gaze at the air above that desk

and see the outline of her arm raised up?

In band, will they hear the sound of one flute gone,

her lips no longer pressed against mouthpiece?

Will the other flutists blow their own breath

out more forcefully to make up for loss?

Will her friends pass along a final note, forgetting

this desk is now empty?

Will the new kid who enters

the room choose that seat, as all eyes follow, as her body lowers

onto the ghost of the girl who came before?

Exit Interview

Kicked out of my house and off the earth,
God's assistant hands me a leaf.
One question is inscribed on the leaf—
Can you define the meaning of your life while on earth?

I banish alliteration and metaphor,
tap my finger on a star, searching
for the brightest truth.

No pen? I ask the faceless assistant.
He hovers above me,
all light and outline; then he points
the arm apparition toward my fingers.

Oh, so that's how it's done here.
I touch one finger to the leaf, aching
for my blue Bic earthbound pens.
This will do, I decide
as light-infused ink spills out of me.

Memory fading, I sift through
bank accounts, purchases, previous jobs,

but all that floods
from me in the end is this—

The weight and wiggle
of my baby after birth,
when he was first cradled in my arms.
From life came life. His adult hand
clutching my dying one at the end.

Stillborn

The milk arrives
to the waiting
lipless air.

A child has come and gone,
off to a lullabyless world
of muted heartbeats,

Born still
into this sterile
silent room.

Family Jewels

Now when she visits
she brings me things—
a ruby pin, a cameo brooch,
wanting to impart jewels
to her daughter
with those still-live hands.

I store these mementos in a tin,
unable to wear them yet.
How can I pin the prospect
of her future death
upon my chest, gold and cameo
reminders of what will soon be gone?

The Moon, My Mother, Loneliness

Tonight we stare at the same
moon, my mother sees time running away—
tiny lights cycling across the darkness,
doused out at the end of sky.

As I get older, the moon grows closer,
the world smaller.

When I was ten, the moon dropped
its golden thread into my bed.

In the late hours of loneliness, moon
comforts me, reveals the bright side,
whispers, *Sometimes I disappear
completely, but I always come back
stronger, brighter.*

Sometimes I am so eclipsed by sadness
I don't even exist,
then I crane my neck
upward and remember moon's words.

My mother beside me tonight, her eyes
smaller, her body depleting, a decade left

at best, maybe two. Perhaps when she

no longer stands here looking up

she'll be pedaling inside the full moon's light,

staring down at me, reeling me slowly

up with that time-lit string.

Leaving Stones

That stone placed
on her Opa's grave
waits between
the wind and the dead.

She watches for a hand
to set the second stone
and listens for the sound
of grief and regret.

The weight of loss
holds her here,
like a paperweight
on top of her chest.

Even though the mourners
have long since gone,
she feels the sharp-edged stone
cutting into her palm.

House on the Hill

God empties the large pail
of grief. It winds through
the village, watery hands
flowing, reaching inside every abode.

Only that house on the hill
sidesteps death. For years
people thought that resident
was a fool—trudging all the way
up the incline with his daily bucket of water
drawn from the town's well
again and again.
                    So many trips.

Now they look up from their newly dug
graves, stare with envy and awe,
closing their hands into fists,
wishing they, too, had built
a house on the hill beyond the clouds,
at the base of sky and foresight.

Vision

When the woman with cancer

floated in that limbo

place between

dying and death,

she asked,

Who is that woman

cloaked in darkness

at the foot of my bed?

Uninvited Guest

The door opens,
but I am not home
to welcome the uninvited guest.

A gust of wind blows,
unlocks my window. At night
birds fly inside my house.

The guest leaves black stones
on the kitchen table
but takes away the silver spoons.

At night I hear the clacking
together of silverware, death's
melody of silver notes rising.

Morning, a bird carries a stone
in its beak, drops it inside
a waiting grave.

Urn

Knocked off the fireplace mantel by the cat, and tired of death, the deceased man in the urn swirled up from the ashes and yawned. Stretching out the gray dusty fragments, he escaped through the chimney and into the clouds. When it rained, he landed in a stream and swam forward with the fish, finally settling inside a minnow.

A boy scooped up the minnow in a plastic bowl and took the fish home. At night, the risen man whispered secrets and advice inside the boy's receptive ears—all he had learned in life and death. The boy grew wise and insightful at a young age.

"Old soul," strangers whispered when the boy looked at them.

Releasing Balloons

Blue helium balloon attached to string
is held by the small hand of a child.
He lets it go on purpose, wants to
know what will happen
then screams when he sees
how far away the elongated circle
of blue is, realizes it will not come back.
The sky swallows objects whole.

It is like this.
You fall in love, think
if I let you go, you will come back
if I want you to.
I am the ruler of the universe.
I can control everyone, everything.
There might be other bright-colored
balloons out there. I am entitled
to variety.

So you get some, the cheerful yellow one,
the pretty pink one, the wild red one.
But you miss that nice blue balloon,
wake up one day, and say

I want that one back,

but by then it is gone,

swallowed whole by the big world.

Final

No more singing

at night

or dreams of falling.

No dreams at all

in fact.

No full wolf moon, quarter moon

or half moon.

Not even a single

charted star.

No changing

burgundy, yellow leaves,

not even a naked

tree. No, no more.

Just blackness upon

blackness upon

blackness.

Unveiling

I wait at my house with hollowed out Jack-o'-lantern
adorned porch steps, while somewhere
children gather their costumes and pillowcases.

Far away, my brothers bend their heads,
stand on autumnal grass and the rabbi recites prayers.
Then my sister-in-law reads a poem she wrote.

My mother sets a stone for me upon the grave.
I set out a candy bowl beside my father's photo
and I wait for trick-or-treaters to arrive.

I watch as darkness lowers its veil,
and no one knocks upon my door, not even ghosts.

Every Poem Is Not About You

When I gave my father my first book
he said, *This is about me, isn't it?*

Of course he did. Center of our universe,
he towered over us four children

from his self-made pedestal, reminded us
for decades *I am God and sun and moon.*

Gone a year. I try to leave him behind
to prove him wrong. He would be

so pleased, laughing even, because here he is
again behind every word and line I pen.

Acknowledgments

The Broad River Review: "What We Bury"

Cairn: "Accidentally Caught in a Funeral Procession"

Connotation Press: "December Shiva," "What They Will Find after He's Gone"

Creosote: "Dust"

Independent Tribune: "Family Jewels"

The Independent Weekly: "Loose Coffins in Carolina"

Nâzim Hikmet Poetry Festival Chapbook: "Unveiling"

News & Observer (Raleigh): "One Year after Your Death"

The Petigru Review: "Merchant Afterlife," "White"

Poetica: "Potato Peel Soup"

RiverSedge: "Box Salesman"

The Sierra Nevada College Review: "Releasing Balloons"

Willard & Maple: "Exit Interview"

Scar Girl chapbook (Finishing Line Press): "Spring Arrives"

Spotlight Anthology (Press 53): "Father-Daughter Dance," "Red," "What They Will Find after He's Gone," "Small Birds at Night," "What We Bury," "Dust," "Loss," "Bats," "One Year after Your Death"

Praying at Coffee Shops chapbook (Main Street Rag): "Dust," "Potato Peel Soup"

About the Author

Maureen A. Sherbondy's poems have appeared in numerous publications, including *Calyx, Feminist Studies, European Judaism, 13th Moon, Comstock Review, Cairn, Crucible, The Roanoke Review,* and the *News & Observer* (Raleigh). Her poems have won first place in The Deane Ritch Lomax Poetry Prize, *The Lyricist* Statewide Poetry Contest, The Carrie McCray Poetry Award, and The Hart Crane Memorial Poetry Award.

Maureen's fiction has won The Piccolo Spoleto Fiction Open. A short story was selected as a runner-up in The William Faulkner–William Wisdom Creative Writing Contest.

Main Street Rag Publishing Company published her first book, *After the Fairy Tale,* (a collection of poetry) in 2007. *Praying at Coffee Shops* was published in 2008. Her short story collection *The Slow Vanishing* was released in 2009. *Weary Blues* was published by Big Table Publishing in 2010.

Maureen lives in Raleigh, NC with her three sons. She has a BA degree from Rutgers University and recently completed her MFA at Queens University of Charlotte. She teaches workshops on publishing and creative writing at various venues. Visit her website at *www.maureensherbondy.com.*

Our Mission

The mission of Brick Road Poetry Press is to publish and promote poetry that entertains, amuses, edifies, and surprises a wide audience of appreciative readers. We are not qualified to judge who deserves to be published, so we concentrate on publishing what we enjoy. Our preference is for poetry geared toward dramatizing the human experience in a language rich with sensory image and metaphor, recognizing that poetry can be, at one and the same time, both familiar as the perspiration of daily labor and outrageous as a carnival sideshow.

Also Available from Brick Road Poetry Press

www.brickroadpoetrypress.com

Dancing on the Rim by Clela Reed

Possible Crocodiles by Barry Marks

Pain Diary by Joseph D. Reich

Otherness by M. Ayodele Heath

Drunken Robins by David Oates

Damnatio Memoriae by Michael Meyerhofer

Lotus Buffet by Rupert Fike

The Melancholy MBA by Richard Donnelly

Two-Star General by Grey Held

Chosen by Toni Thomas

Etch and Blur by Jamie Thomas

Water-Rites by Ann E. Michael

Bad Behavior by Michael Steffen

BRICK ROAD

POETRY PRESS

About the Prize

The Brick Road Poetry Prize, established in 2010, is awarded annually for the best book-length poetry manuscript. Entries are accepted August 1st through November 1st. The winner receives $1000 and publication. For details on our preferences and the complete submission guidelines, please visit our website at www.brickroadpoetrypress.com.

17364833R00066

Made in the USA
Charleston, SC
07 February 2013